MW01152779

ASK someone GRUMPY to READ you this BOOK

words & design by
Matt Roemisch
—— with ——
Jenni Roemisch

edited by
Jennifer Mansker

A "Read Together" book.

Ask someone grumpy to read you this book.
Really... *ask them!*

Insight from the Author:

Ok, ok - I'll admit it! I know a thing or two about being grumpy. Although I was grumpy before (for sure), I've been extra grumpy while writing this book. *Ask Someone Grumpy to Read You This Book* was written during the great quarantine of 2020. As a husband and father, I was concerned about keeping my family well and safe. As an elementary school teacher, I was worried about all my "school kids" too. I was also feeling the stress and strain of other families and people around the world. It was such an immediate and sustained change from our everyday lives that I know my grumpiness presented itself, front and center. I needed to write this book - *so that I could read it!*

"He who began a good work in you will carry it on to completion..." - Philippians 1:6

This book is dedicated to my wife and two sons that have to put up with my grumpy self on a daily basis. You guys are amazing, and I wouldn't want to be stuck at home with anyone else. I love y'all!

Copyright © 2020 Matt Roemisch | Abilene, Texas, USA | First Print Edition May 2020

ISBN 978-0-578-67710-1 (paperback book) | Library of Congress Control Number: 2020906596

Words Written by Matt Roemisch with Jenni Roemisch
Edited by Jennifer Mansker
Cover Design / Book Layout by Matt Roemisch
Cover & Character Illustrations Licensed from Getty (CSA Images)

MattRoemisch.com | AskSomeoneGrumpy.com

GRUMPY (adjective):

A **grouchy** word used to describe
someone who is in a **lousy** mood.
They might even be angry, sad,
or just have a **terrible** attitude.

First things, first.

If you are reading this book
by yourself, stop right now!
Did you even read the title?
It tells you exactly how.

You must ask someone grumpy
to read you this book.
If you can't find someone grumpy,

just take a
second look.

Trust me,
grumpy people are all around,
so jump up and find one,
then come sit back down.

STOP!

Do not turn the page.
Do not even pretend to look.

Unless...

you are the grumpy one,
asked to read the words in this book.

Oh, hello there.

To you, the grumpy person
who is reading these very words.
You have been carefully selected,
your grouchy look, preferred.

To you, who is listening
and hearing my grumpy tone.
Is it my face, my words,
or because I want to be all alone?

Why do you think
I am grumpy?

Is my forehead all scrunched up?
Am I frowning or looking sad?

Are my eyebrows laying low

and showing that I am mad?

Am I acting cranky or crabby?

Am I being snippy with my words?
Do I sound cantankerous or grumbly,
or crotchety and absurd?

Was I sitting by myself with a
scowl upon my face?
Why are you so close to me?
This is my personal space!

Ughhhh!

Even if I wasn't before...

Now I am Grumpy!

So now, I want you to listen,
and understand

why I might
feel this way.

It may not be because I'm angry
or just having a really bad day.

Sometimes, I might be grumpy
because I didn't get enough sleep.
Or maybe I'm just hungry
and need something good to eat.

Maybe
I just heard

some upsetting or bad news.
Perhaps I'm feeling sick,
or I'm worried about you.

Usually, my grumpy mood
belongs to me and not you.
You have done nothing wrong,

I'm just feeling kind of blue.

You probably knew
that I was grumpy,
because you could
see it on my face.

A face tells all sorts of stories.

It shows feelings, so just in case...

You need to know the power
that you hide inside your face!

It is full of muscles and strings,
that control your every look.

So show me a

BIG smile :)

as I keep reading you this book.

I want you to grin as big
as you possibly can!

Your smile makes me feel better,

and that's your number one plan.

When I am feeling down
and need some cheering up.
Your actions are important,
so maybe ask me,

"What's up?"

Sometimes, when I'm grumpy,

I want to be left alone. It's true.
But other times I need a friend,
and that friend just might be you.

Do you think we need some chocolate,
yummy ice cream or french fries?

Or maybe I
just need a hug,

or for you to sit here by my side.

Let's listen to some awesome music!

Groovy tunes can change my vibe.
We could watch some funny videos,
and don't forget to hit subscribe!

Going outside to run and play
is also a fantastic trick.
Fresh air and fun-filled exercise,

will cheer me up
real quick.

Sharing silly stories or
great memories can also be,
a great way to show empathy
between you and grumpy me.

Oh, wait. Oh, wait.

I feel a change!

What's happening to me?
Reading with you has fixed my frown,
I think I'm starting to be...

I am, I am!

I'm starting to be the opposite of grumpy.

Can't you see? My face has changed,

I'm smiling now.

I'm happy!

HAPPY (adjective):

A **lively** word used to describe
someone who is in a **good** mood.
No longer feeling grumpy
but full of **gratitude**. Thank you!

CPSIA information can be obtained
at www.ICGtesting.com
Printed in the USA
LVHW021115170520
655785LV00002B/100

9 780578 677101